Practise your Prepositions

L.L. Keane

Longman

Contents

Introduction

Introduction

1 This book groups prepositions into seven sets, as follows:
   1 Position (Units 1–3)
   2 Direction (Units 5–7)
   3 Time (Units 9–10)
   4 Description (Units 12–13)
   5 Adjective + preposition combinations (Units 15–17)
   6 Verb + preposition combinations (Units 19–22)
   7 Usual phrases (Units 24–26)

2 Each unit is two pages.

3 Each set of presentation units (e.g. Units 1–3) is followed by a
   Mixed Practice Unit (e.g. Unit 4). These Mixed Practice Units
   revise the prepositions taught in the set, and usually contain
   some exercises which are more demanding than those in the
   presentation units.

4 Each presentation unit is self-contained, and therefore these
   units can be done in any order. It is only necessary to read the
   information on page 5 before starting.

5 All the work is practised in meaningful contexts, and much of it
   deals with the four young people introduced on page 5.

6 Many units end with a relatively open-ended exercise, in which
   students can use the language taught to talk or write about
   themselves, or to exchange information and ideas with a
   partner.

7 It is possible to use this book for class work, homework, or –
   since it has a Key – for self-access study.

Tina is a student. She is twenty years old.

Paul is Tina's brother. He is seventeen years old and is still at school.

Ted is a photographer for British Tourist Books.

Sue is an editor in the same company.

Tina, Paul, Ted and Sue are going to travel round England together. They are going to prepare information and pictures for a book called *Young People's Action Holidays in England*.

1 Where? 1

1 The office of British Tourist Books is *in* Regent Street. It is *at* 22 Regent Street, *in* a large building called Tourism House. This is *near* Piccadilly Circus, but rather *far from* Oxford Circus. Tourism House is *on the corner of* Carlton Street. There is a cinema *opposite* it and a bank *next to* it.

■ Where is the office of (a) Japanese Airlines Ltd and (b) the Austrian National Tourist Office?
Use the words below:

in	at	near	far from	on the corner of
opposite	next to			

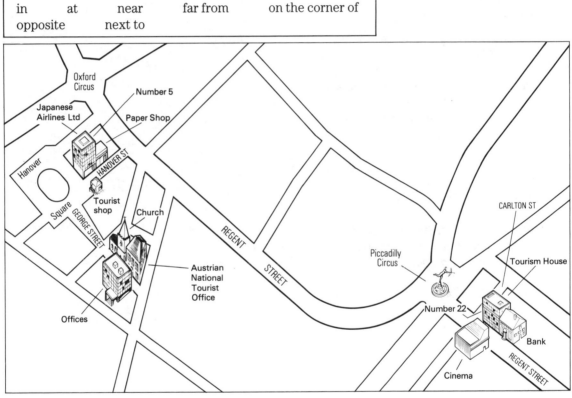

Japanese Airlines Ltd is ¹ __near__ Oxford Circus. The office is

² _____ Hanover Square, ³ _____ 5 Hanover Square,

to be exact. It is ⁴ _____ Hanover Street. There is a paper

shop ⁵ _____ it, and a tourist shop ⁶ _____ it. Japanese

Airlines Ltd is rather ⁷ _____ Piccadilly Circus.

The Austrian National Tourist Office is not ⁸ _____ the

Japanese Airlines office. It is ⁹ _____ 30 St George Street.

There is a church ¹⁰ _____ it, and some

offices ¹¹ _____ it.

2 Sue is talking to Tina on the telephone.
'So you and Paul can come on Tuesday! Good!
Now, our offices are *in* Tourism House. We're
on the second floor. The Regency Restaurant is
above us. It's *at the top of* Tourism House, and
we're just *below* it. You'll recognise the building
easily; there are some flags *on top of* it.'

REGENCY
RESTAURANT

BRITISH
TOURIST
BOOKS

TED'S FLAT

PETER'S FLAT

BLAKE HOUSE

COFFEE SHOP

Where is Ted's flat?
Use the words from column 2 in column 3. Cross out each word in
column 2 when you use it.

Column 1	**Column 2**	**Column 3**	**Column 4**
1 Ted's flat is	on	*in*	Blake House.
2 There are some TV aerials	~~in~~	_____	the building.
3 Ted's flat is	above	_____	the third floor.
4 It is	below	_____	the building.
5 It is	on top of	_____	a coffee shop.
6 Peter's flat is	at the top of	_____	Ted's flat.

2 Where? 2

Sue is planning a photo for the book. She has made a drawing and is talking to Ted about it. 'Let's have the Landrover *on the left of* the picture, Tina and Paul *in the middle of* the picture, you *on the right* and all the luggage and equipment *at the front*. And we can have the entrance to Tourism House *at the back of* the picture.'

But Ted has a different idea. He says:

'How about having the Landrover ¹ ___in the middle of___

the picture, with some trees ² _____ it?

Then we can have Paul ³ _____ , Tina

⁴ _____ the picture, and the luggage

somewhere ⁵ _____ .'

Then Sue has another idea. She says:

'Let's have Tina *inside* the Landrover, and Paul *outside* it, standing *beside* it. We can have you *in front of* the Landrover, taking a picture. The luggage can be *round* Paul. And we'll have Tourism House *behind* you all.'

Now describe the final picture!

Ted was ¹ ___inside___ the Landrover, and Tina and Paul

were ² _____ it. The luggage was

³ _____ Tina, who was standing

⁴ _____ the Landrover. Paul was sitting on the

ground ⁵ _____ it, and ⁶ _____ them

all there were some trees.

3 This is Paul's room. He is sitting *in* an armchair, and his guitar is *on* a small chair. He has several pictures *on* the wall, and there are some pictures *on* the ceiling, *above* his bed. He is packing for his trip with British Tourist Books, so his bag is *in a corner of* the room. Some of his clothes are *on* the floor. You can see a tree *through* the window.

■ Now complete this description of Tina's room.

Tina has several pictures

1_____ **on** _____ the walls of her room,

but she has none 2_____ the

ceiling. There is a lamp 3_____

her bed. 4_____ the window,

you can see a roof. Tina's bag is

5_____ the floor, there are

some books 6_____ a chair,

and her tennis racquet is

7_____ the room. The family's

cat is sleeping 8_____ the

armchair.

4 What about you?

Where is your home? Write about its location, using words from page 6.

_____

_____

_____

_____

5 Now write about a room that you know; for example, your bedroom, a classroom, or the office of a member of your family. Describe its location and some of the things in it. Use words from pages 7 and 9.

_____

_____

_____

_____

9

3 Where? 3

1 Portsmouth is a town *in* England. It is *in the south of* England, and it is *on* the coast. *Off* the coast, near Portsmouth, there is an island called the Isle of Wight. This island is *south of* Portsmouth. It is famous for watersports. Tina and Paul are staying *in* St Helen's, which is *in the east of* the island. St Helen's is about ten kilometres *from* Portsmouth.

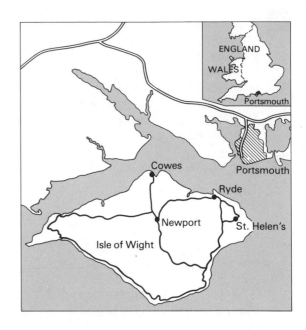

True or false?
Write ✓ after the true statements, and × after the false statements. Correct the false statements.
1 Portsmouth is in the north of St Helen's.
2 Newport is west of St Helen's.
3 Cowes is in the north of the Isle of Wight.
4 Portsmouth is off the coast of England.
5 Cowes is south of Newport.

_____

_____

_____

2 Complete the description.

Majorca is an island ¹____off____ the coast

of Spain. It is ²_____ of Valencia,

which is a large town ³_____ Spain.

Palma is ⁴_____ the coast of Majorca.

Many tourists come and stay ⁵_____

Palma. Soller is ⁶_____ of Palma. It is

about sixteen kilometres ⁷_____

Palma. Soller is ⁸_____ of Majorca.

3 Sue, Paul and Ted are talking about the sorts of places that they like for their holidays.

SUE: I like climbing, so I like a place *in* the mountains.
PAUL: Well, I like swimming, so I like a place that's *on* the sea, or *on* a lake or *on* a river. Of course, if the weather's cold, I don't swim *in* the sea or the lake, but I like being near water.
TED: Well, I like a quiet holiday. I don't like a place that's *on* a busy road.

■ Write *in* or *on* in column 2.

1 London is	_*on*_	the River Thames.
2 There are fish	_____	the River Thames.
3 Quito is	_____	the Andes Mountains.
4 Chicago is	_____	Lake Michigan.
5 New York is	_____	the Atlantic Ocean.
6 People swim	_____	the Mediterranean Sea.
7 Ryde is	_____	the road from St Helen's to Cowes.

4 Complete the sentences.

Tina, Paul, Ted and Sue stayed in hostels in many different places.
Paul liked hostel C, because it was ¹___*by*___ a river, and
hostel D because it was ²_____ a lake. Sue liked hostel A
because it was ³_____ a mountain, and she liked hostel B
even better, because it was right ⁴_____ a mountain. Ted
liked hostel F, because it was ⁵_____ the road, hostel E
because it was ⁶_____ a wood, and of course he liked
hostels A and B too, because they were ⁷_____ the road.

4 Mixed practice

1 Complete the street plan.

Read the description below, and draw the symbols in their correct position.

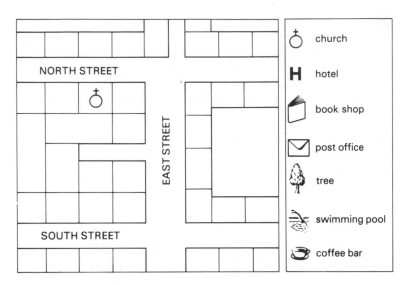

There is a church in North Street. Next to the church, west of it, there is a hotel. Also next to the church, on the corner of East Street, there is a book shop. Next to the book shop, just south of it, there is a post office. In front of the post office there is a tree, and behind the post office there is a swimming pool. Opposite the post office there is a coffee bar.

2 How has this shop window changed?

Describe the differences.

In A the name is ,¹_____ of the window, but in B it is ²_____ of it.

In A, the cupboard is ³_____ of the display, but in B it is ⁴_____ of it.

In A, the hat is ⁵_____ the cupboard, but in B it is ⁶_____ it.

In A, the shirt is ⁷_____ the lamp, but in B it is ⁸_____ it.

In A, the goggles are ⁹_____ the bowl, but in B they are ¹⁰_____

3 Write *one* word in each blank.

This is the entrance to Western Recording
Studios Ltd. The receptionist is sitting
¹ **on** her chair, with a lamp
² _____ her. There is a clock
³ _____ the wall ⁴ _____ her, and a
tall plant in a pot stands ⁵ _____ the floor.
A visitor is sitting ⁶ _____ an armchair.
The studios are ⁷ _____ 53 Alexandra
Street, ⁸ _____ the seventh floor.

Elba is an island ⁹ _____ the coast of Italy.
It is only about two kilometres ¹⁰ _____
the Italian coast, so it is very ¹¹ _____ the
coast. Elba is 240 kilometres ¹² _____
Genoa, so it is rather ¹³ _____ _____
Genoa. Genoa is ¹⁴ _____ the coast. It is
¹⁵ _____ of Elba, and is
¹⁶ _____ _____ _____
_____ Italy.

4 Answer these questions, or ask a partner to answer them.
If you could choose ...

What city, town, village or island would you live in? _____

Describe its location. _____

_____

Where would your house or flat be? _____

_____

How would you arrange your favourite room? _____

_____

_____

Where would you go for your next holiday? _____

Describe the location of this place. _____

_____

5 Direction 1

1 Tina and Paul are in Brighton, in the Tourist Information Centre. An assistant is telling them the way from the Centre to the Dome Concert Hall. 'When you leave this building, turn right *into* Barton Street. Turn *right* again *into* East Street. Go *along* East Street *as far as* North Street. Cross North Street, and go *past* the Royal Pavilion, continuing *towards* Victoria Gardens. Turn *left into* Church Street and there's the Dome.'

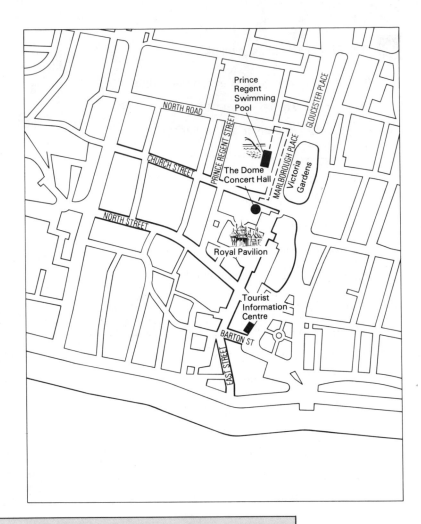

I turned/ran *into* Barton Street (= I ENTERED BARTON STREET FROM ANOTHER STREET)

I was running *in* Barton Street (= I WAS ALREADY IN BARTON STREET, AND I WAS RUNNING IN IT)

---

2 Complete the description of Paul and Tina's walk from the Dome. It follows the dotted line on the map. Write *one* word in each blank.

Paul and Tina walked ¹___**to**___ The Prince Regent

Swimming Pool ²_____ the Dome. They crossed Church

Street and went ³_____ Marlborough Place, ⁴_____

Gloucester Place. They walked ⁵_____ Victoria Gardens

and continued ⁶_____ _____ _____ North

Road. Then they turned ⁷_____ ⁸_____ North Road,

and found the swimming pool on their left.

2 Paul was staying in an old hotel and couldn't find his room.
Complete the sentences.

The lift stopped *at* the third ¹ **floor** .

Paul got *out of* the ² _____ ,

and went *up* some ³ _____ .

Then he went *down* some ⁴ _____ .

He walked *along* a ⁵ _____ ,

through a ⁶ _____ ,

and *into* a ⁷ _____ !

The room is He lives	*on* the third floor.	The lift stopped He got out	*at* the third floor.

3 Tina couldn't find her room either. She walked:

¹ **out of** the dining room,

² _____ some stairs,

³ _____ a passage,

⁴ _____ the lounge,

⁵ _____ the lounge,

⁶ _____ some stairs,

⁷ _____ an arch,

and then ⁸ _____ the dining room again!

6 Direction 2

| across | 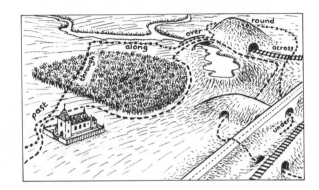 | something flat (e.g. a road or a railway line) |

across ⟶ something flat (e.g. a road or a railway line)

over ⌒ if the path or road goes up and then down (e.g. because of a hill or a bridge)

through 🌿→ something that rises on both sides (e.g. tall grass, a wood, a town)

The dotted line (.....) shows a path in the country. Describe where it goes.

The path goes ¹ __*past*__ a church,
² _____ a wood, ³ _____ part of a
river, ⁴ _____ a bridge, ⁵ _____ a
hill, ⁶ _____ a railway line, and
⁷ _____ a road.

But Tina and Paul went a different way. The broken line
(– – – – –) shows where they went. Describe their walk.

They went ¹ __*past*__ the church, ² _____ the wood,
³ _____ the bridge, ⁴ _____ a stream, ⁵ _____ a
tunnel, ⁶ _____ a road, and ⁷ _____ a railway line.

3

off

off
(a) from a flat surface, e.g. a table or a hard chair.
(b) down from, e.g. a roof.

out of

out of
from inside something, e.g. a box or an armchair.

on to

on to
from a place to a surface, e.g. a table or a hard chair.

into

into
from one place to the inside of another, e.g. a room or some water.

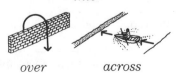
over   *across*

over/across
from one side to the other. Usually *over* if you go up and then
down, e.g. to climb *over* a wall.

■ Paul was at an adventure camp. Fill in the blanks to say where he went.

Paul fell ¹___off___ a bridge ²_____ a river. He swam

³_____ the river, then climbed ⁴_____ it, and

climbed ⁵_____ some rocks. He ran ⁶_____ a field

and jumped ⁷_____ a gate. There were some bulls in that

field, so he climbed ⁸_____ a pile of stones, and then

jumped ⁹_____ the stones, ¹⁰_____ the ground on

the other side of the fence.

7 Direction 3

1

		A town or village	A country
She flew/went/ travelled, etc. She came She got (INFORMAL)	*to*	Oxford	England
She left	*for*		
She arrived	*in*	Oxford (IN A PART OF THE TOWN)	England (WE THINK OF THE PLACE AS AN AREA WHICH SURROUNDS A PERSON.)
She arrived (NEVER: She arrived ⱵⱵ)	*at*	Oxford (e.g. BY TRAIN, AT THE STATION)	Bahrain (WE THINK OF THE PLACE AS A POINT ON A JOURNEY. NOTE THAT WE DO NOT USE AT FOR LARGER COUNTRIES.)

These are some of Marco Polo's travels from Venice.
Write *at, in, to* or *for* in column 2.

1 In 1271 Marco Polo left   __*for*__   Persia.

2 Some time later he arrived   _____   China.

3 In 1272 he got   _____   Tibet.

4 In 1292 he went   _____   India.

5 In about 1294 he went back   _____   Persia.

6 He arrived   _____   Tabriz in 1294 or 1295.

7 At the end of 1295 he came back   _____   Venice.

2 A young tennis player is telling Tina about her travels.
Write *in, at, to* or *for*.

'Last year I went [1]__*to*__ about twenty different countries. I

went [2]_____ Japan for the first time. I came [3]_____

England for the first time in 1985. We had rather a difficult

journey this time. Our plane arrived [4]_____ Manchester at

2.00 p.m., but our luggage only got [5]_____ Manchester

three hours later. The car from the airport broke down, so we

arrived [6]_____ Manchester itself several hours late. The

next day we left [7]_____ London, and arrived [8]_____

Heathrow Airport without any problems, luckily.'

3 Look at the map and read about Tina and Paul's bicycle ride.

One day, Tina and Paul cycled from West Dean to Stonehenge. First they cycled north, *as far as* The Common. Then they cycled West *towards* Salisbury, going *through* Winterslow, and continued *as far as* Winterbourne. It was about 10.00 a.m. when they cycled *into* Winterbourne, so they had a cup of coffee there. They were cycling *out of* Winterbourne when Tina had a puncture.

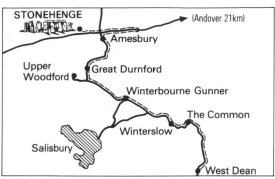

They cycled *out of/into* West Dean (IF WE THINK OF THIS PLACE AS AN AREA)
They cycled *from/to* West Dean (IF WE THINK OF THIS PLACE AS A POINT ON A JOURNEY)

■ Complete the description of Tina and Paul's bicycle ride, using prepositions from the passage and table above.

After Tina and Paul had mended the puncture, they cycled

west, ¹ *towards* Upper Woodford. But then they turned

north and went ² _____ _____

_____ Great Durnford. They continued

³ _____ Great Durnford, and were cycling

⁴ _____ Amesbury when Paul had a puncture. So it was

11.30 when they at last cycled ⁵ _____

_____ Amesbury; then they took a wrong turning, and

began cycling ⁶ _____ Andover. Altogether, the ride

⁷ _____ Stonehenge ⁸ _____ West Dean

took them nearly four hours.

4 Describe an interesting journey – real or imaginary – in your country or abroad. Use these verbs (in any order), with a suitable preposition after each one:

travelled	left	arrived	came	got	went

_____

_____

_____

_____

19

8 Mixed practice

1 Every year, about 17,000 people run a distance of 42 kilometres in the London Marathon.
Complete this description of the route, using the prepositions below:

along through past towards as far as round over into across

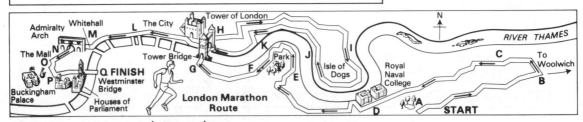

A–B The route goes ¹ _towards_ Woolwich, then turns and goes back

C–D ² _____ Greenwich, going

D   ³ _____ the Royal Naval College.

E–F It goes ⁴ _____ a park,

G–H ⁵ _____ Tower Bridge, ⁶ _____ the River Thames,

I–J ⁷ _____ a district called the Isle of Dogs, then

K–L ⁸ _____ the River Thames, going ⁹ _____ the financial district (called
     'The City').

M   It turns ¹⁰ _____ Whitehall, and

N   goes ¹¹ _____ Admiralty Arch.

N–O It goes ¹² _____ The Mall, ¹³ _____ Buckingham Palace.

P   Then it turns ¹⁴ _____ Birdcage Walk, going ¹⁵ _____ the river again.

P–Q It goes ¹⁶ _____ the Houses of Parliament, and ¹⁷ _____ Westminster
     Bridge, ¹⁸ _____ the east side of the bridge, where the Marathon finishes.

2 Describe the burglar's actions, using the prepositions below:

into in on to on out of from off up down over across through towards

  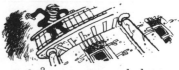

He climbed ¹ _up_ a
drainpipe,

² _____ a railing,

and ³ _____ a balcony.

Then he got ⁴_____ a bedroom, ⁵_____ an open window.

There he found a necklace ⁶_____ a drawer.

He took some rings ⁷_____ a box,

and two candlesticks ⁸_____ a small table.

(All this time he had been walking ⁹_____ a carpet that was connected to a burglar alarm.)

Then he slid ¹⁰_____ the drainpipe,

ran ¹¹_____ the house

¹²_____ a lawn,

¹³_____ a bank, and

¹⁴_____ the arms of a policeman.

3 In column 3, write the correct preposition from column 2.

1 They came	at	_to_	Paris last week.
2 They arrived	for	_____	France a month ago.
3 Next, they're going	in	_____	Japan.
4 They're leaving	to	_____	Japan on Tuesday.
5 They're going		_____	Tokyo.
6 They'll arrive		_____	Tokyo on Wednesday.
7 They'll come back		_____	France next month.

9 When? 1

<table>
<tr><td>in</td><td>1989 (= A YEAR)
(the) winter (= A SEASON)
April (= A MONTH)</td><td>on</td><td>Friday (= A DAY OF THE WEEK)
New Year's Day/my birthday (= A PARTICULAR DAY)
8 April (= A DATE)</td></tr>
<tr><td colspan="4">**Note** We say *in* April, but *on* 8 April.</td></tr>
<tr><td>at</td><td colspan="3">Easter/Eid (= A RELIGIOUS PERIOD)</td></tr>
</table>

Complete this summary of events in Brighton.

[1] **In**_____ 1987, there were many public events in Brighton [2]_____ the spring. For example, [3]_____ Easter there was a carnival (it was [4]_____ Monday 20 April), and [5]_____ May there were three big events. [6]_____ the summer and autumn there were fewer events. There was a fishing boat race [7]_____ a Saturday [8]_____ July, a tennis tournament [9]_____ October, and a race for vintage cars from London [10]_____ 7 November. Of course, there were many parties and dances [11]_____ 31 December and [12]_____ New Year's Day. The programme of public events was similar [13]_____ 1988.

Some events in 1987 — BRIGHTON

Motorcycle race
Sat. 21 March

Easter carnival
Mon. 20 April

Festival of the arts
Sat. 2 – Sun. 17 May

Fireworks
Sat. 9 May

Boat show
Wed. 6 – Sun. 10 May

Fishing boat race
Sat. 18 July

Tennis tournament
Sat. 17 – Sat. 31 October

Vintage car race from London
Sat. 7 November

> There are no prepositions before *last, next, this* and *every*:
>   There were many events in Brighton *last year*.
>   There's a carnival *next Monday*. It's taking place *this month*. It happens *every year*.

Paul is writing to a friend. In each blank, write a preposition or put a dash (−).

I'm sorry we weren't here ¹___*in*___ May! There aren't so

many events ²_____ this month, but there's a fishing boat

race ³_____ next Saturday. ⁴_____ Friday we're

going riding. (Do you remember? I had some riding lessons

⁵_____ last summer.) I'd like to be here ⁶_____

October, when there's a big tennis tournament. They have the

tournament ⁷_____ every October.

in the morning/evening (= A PART OF A DAY)	*at* 6 o'clock/midday (= A TIME)

Here is the next part of Paul's letter. In each blank, write *in, at* or put a dash (−).

Yesterday we went to a sports centre ¹___*in*___ the morning.
We started playing table tennis ²_____ 10 o'clock, had
lunch ³_____ 12 o'clock, and ⁴_____ the afternoon
we played basketball and then swam. ⁵_____ the evening
we went to a disco, and I got to bed ⁶_____ 2 o'clock in the
morning.

   After breakfast ⁷_____ this morning we hired bikes and
biked round Brighton. We're having a rest now, but ⁸_____
this evening we're going to a concert, which begins ⁹_____
8.30.

10 When? 2

1 Tina's life

1968	Born in Oxford.
1970	Brother Paul born.
1972	Family moved to London.
1973	Tina started school.
1979	Moved to secondary school.
1981	Started guitar lessons.
1985	Passed school leaving exam. Then worked in a shop.
1986	Began university.
1988	Still at university. Still plays the guitar.

Examples
Tina lived in Oxford *from* 1968 *to/until/till* (INFORMAL) 1972.
She was born *before* Paul.
She started school *after* her fifth birthday.
In 1986, she had been playing the guitar *for* five years.
She had been playing it *since* 1981.
She began playing it *during* her school days.

Notes
We use *for* with periods which we measure or count:
  for five years/four weeks/three days/two minutes
We use *during* with periods which we do **not** measure or count:
  during lunch/her school days/1986
We use *since* with a point in time:
  since 1986/last March/six o'clock

Complete these statements about Tina's life. Imagine that it is now 1988.

1 Tina lived in Oxford ___for___ two years.

2 She has lived in London _____ sixteen years.

3 She has lived there _____ 1972.

4 She started school _____ the family's move to London.

5 She attended her secondary school _____ 1979

_____ 1985.

6 She worked in a shop _____ her summer holidays.

7 She worked there _____ three months.

8 She has been at university _____ two years.

9 She has been playing the guitar _____ seven years.

10 She has been playing it _____ 1981.

> Tina was at school *from* 1973 *to/until/till* 1985.
> She was at school *until/till* (NOT ⊠) June 1985.
> She had left school *by* July 1985. (*by* = BEFORE, NOT LATER THAN)

Use each preposition from column 2 in column 3.
Cross out each word in column 2 when you use it.

1 Tina lived in Oxford	to	*until*	1972.
2 She had started school	to	_____	her sixth birthday.
3 She worked in a shop from July 1985	by	_____	October 1985.
4 She'll stay at university	by	_____	June 1989.
5 She'll leave university	by	_____	the autumn of 1989.
6 She says she's going to work hard	~~until~~	_____	the final examination!
7 She'll forget this promise	until	_____	next weekend.
8 Last night she danced from ten p.m.	until	_____	two in the morning.

Answer these questions, or ask your partner to answer them. Use the prepositions in italics in your answers.

1 *For* how long have you lived in your present home?

I have lived in my present home ___ *for* _____

2 So that is *since* when?

That's since _____

3 *Since* when have you been learning English?

_____

4 *Until* what date are you going to attend English classes?

_____

5 *By* what date will you stop studying altogether?

_____

11 Mixed practice

1 At a travel agent's.
Write a suitable preposition in each blank.

'Right! your plane leaves ¹__*at*__ 14.00 hours. You should

check in 1½ hours ²_____ departure time, so you need to

be at the airport ³_____ 12.30. You can wait in the

departure lounge ⁴_____ check-in time ⁵_____

departure time.

You'll probably wait there ⁶_____ about 13.50. Now,

about getting to the airport. There's an airport bus that leaves the

terminal ⁷_____ 11.00 hours. You could catch that. I know

there's always a lot of traffic going to the airport ⁸_____

the morning, ⁹_____ about 8.00 ¹⁰_____ about

10.00. However, you'll be going ¹¹_____ that period, so

you'll be O.K.'

2 In a coffee bar.
Write a dash (–) or one of the prepositions below in each space:

from	for	during	since	to	until/till

'Where have you been? We agreed to meet at 2.30. I've been

waiting for you ¹__*for*__ hours! Well, not exactly hours,

but ²_____ 2.35. Let me see – ³_____ 2.35

⁴_____ now: that's forty minutes. I've drunk three cups of

coffee ⁵_____ that time and got very bored. If I'd brought

a book I could at least have been reading ⁶_____ forty

minutes. Anyway, what's your excuse?'

'My excuse? I've been waiting for you ⁷_____ thirty

minutes, in the street. We agreed to meet on the street corner,

didn't we? Anyway, ⁸_____ next week let's meet

⁹_____ Tuesday. That's easier for me than Wednesday. See

you ¹⁰_____ next Tuesday, then.'

'What? Are you going already? Aren't you going to stay

11_____ a few minutes?'

'No, I can't! I've got the dentist 12_____ this

afternoon. I'll have to wait 13_____ Tuesday for your news!'

3 A reporter has been interviewing a pop star and has made these notes. Use the notes to write his article. The date of the article is 10 April 1988.

> **Contessa**
>
> 10.5.63 Born in Leeds.
> 1968 - 79 School (hated it).
> 1973 Began singing in church choir (left 1978).
> 1978 Had already made 3 records! (for church).
> 1980 Began singing with local group.
>   (The Pebbles). (Left group 1982).
> 4.8.81 Sang in show in Brighton. Mammoth
>   Records producer in audience.
> Two weeks later: signed contract with Mammoth
> Records. Still under contract with Mammoth.
> 1986 + 1987 : Golden discs.
> Says: 'Have been singing for other people 15
> years, but really sing for myself.'
> Plans to make third gold disc ('not later than
> 25th birthday'!) Checked charts last Saturday
> - seems possible.

_____

_____

_____

_____

_____

_____

_____

_____

_____

12 How?

1 Ways of travelling

In general		When talking about particular vehicles
by	bike/motorbike/car/ van/lorry/train/plane/ air/bus/tram/ship	on his/that, etc. bike/motorbike in my/this, etc. car/van/lorry on[1] the train/plane/bus/tram/ship
	boat	on the boat (if a large boat) in the boat (if a small boat)
on	foot	

Examples
I like travelling *by* bike.
I travelled around Italy *on my cousin's* bike.

Note
[1]It is possible, but less usual, to say *in* the train, etc.

Ted is talking about a holiday which he had once in the United States.
Write prepositions from the table above in these blanks, adding other words if necessary (e.g. *the, a*).

In New York I went around ¹___*on*___ foot mainly. You can visit the Statue of Liberty ²_____ boat, and ³_*on the*_ boat I met another Englishman. We decided to go together to San Francisco ⁴_____ bus, because it's cheaper than going ⁵_____ train or ⁶_____ plane. Altogether we spent four days and nights ⁷_____ bus. We wanted to go round San Francisco ⁸_____ car; a cousin of mine lent me his car, but after we'd been ⁹_____ car for only a few hours, it broke down. By this time it was midnight, and we started to go back to my cousin's house ¹⁰_____ foot, but a lorry-driver stopped and took us back ¹¹_____ lorry. I came back to London ¹²_____ air, and I can tell you I was too tired to talk to anyone ¹³_____ plane! I think it would be great to do the trip from New York to San Francisco ¹⁴_____ motorbike. There's a book about a man who took his small son right across the States ¹⁵_____ old motorbike.

2 How things are made

Things can be made ...

Of MATERIALS OR SUBSTANCES: This table is made *of* wood.
out of A COMPLETELY DIFFERENT THING (one object is changed into another): She is making a dress for her daughter *out of* some old curtains.
by PEOPLE: The Pyramids were built *by* people who lived a long time ago.
with (= using) TOOLS AND OTHER AIDS: On the beach we built sandcastles *with* our buckets and spades.

In Brighton, our four friends made their own costumes for a fancy-dress disco.
Read the first description. Then complete the other descriptions, using the correct prepositions.

Safety pins

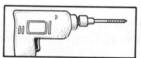
glue

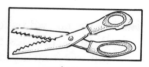
drill

scissors

Paul's crown

This crown is made *of* cardboard. The jewels on it are made *out of* sweets. It was made *by* Paul. Paul stuck on the sweets *with* glue.

Tina's dress

This dress is made ¹_____ a rubbish bag, which is made ²_____ black plastic. The dress was made ³_____ Tina. She cut out the armholes and neck line ⁴_____ some special scissors.

Ted's 'musical instrument'

This 'musical instrument' was made ⁵_____ Ted. It is made ⁶_____ a long stick, some pieces of wire and some bottle tops. The bottle tops are made ⁷_____ metal, so they make a noise. Ted made the holes in them ⁸_____ a drill.

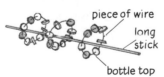
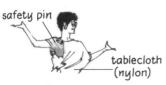

Sue's dress

This dress is made ⁹_____ two table cloths. They are made ¹⁰_____ nylon, so it's rather hot. It was made ¹¹_____ Sue. She put it together ¹²_____ safety pins.

13 What are they like?

1 He/She is a person . . .

_of_[1] (AGE)	_with_ (PHYSICAL CHARACTERISTICS)
about 20 about 16 at least 25 about 18	a big smile an amazing hairstyle curly hair a small moustache
[1]**Note** Do not use 'years' or 'years old' after _of_.	

_in_ (THINGS WE WEAR)	_with_ (THINGS WE CARRY)
a small black hat dark glasses a white blouse a football shirt	a funny football a strange bag a walking stick a guitar

At the fancy dress disco.
Read the first description. Then describe the other people, using phrases from the table.

A man _of_ about 20, _with_ a big smile, _in_ a football shirt and _with_ a funny football.

A girl of [1]about 18 , with [2]_____ , in [3]_____ , and with [4]_____ .

A man of [5]_____ , with [6]_____ , in [7]_____ , and with [8]_____ .

A girl of [9]_____ , in [10]_____ , with [11]_____ and with [12]_____ .

2

as (FOR A PERSON'S JOB OR ROLE)	*like* (TO COMPARE THINGS)
She works *as a reporter*.	She ran *like the wind*.
He joined the team *as an extra player*.	He looks *like his father*.

Note
You must use *a/an* before the name of a job:
   She works *as a reporter* (not 'as reporter')

Things that people said at the disco.
Write *as* or *like*.

1 TINA: 'Goodness! You look ^{1} <u>like</u> Charlie Chaplin. And you dance ^{2}_____ him too!'

2 TED: 'I went to the United States ^{3}_____ a student. I managed to look ^{4}_____ an
         American, but of course I didn't sound ^{5}_____ one.'

3 SUE: 'I can't dance all night ^{6}_____ you! I'm not here ^{7}_____ a tourist, you know!
         I'm working. Anyway, I'll sleep ^{8}_____ a baby tonight!'

4 PAUL: 'Ted's with us ^{9}_____ our photographer. I'd like to take photos ^{10}_____ his!
          His camera's ^{11}_____ a computer!'

3 Using *of, with* and *in*.

1 Describe yourself: your age, a physical characteristic,
   something you are wearing, and something you are holding or
   using.

I am a man/woman/boy/girl _____

_____

_____

_____

_____

2 Describe someone in your class in the same way. Ask your
   neighbour to guess whom you have described.

_____

_____

_____

_____

_____

14 Mixed practice

1 Three presents.
Write *as, like, of, out of* or *by* in the blanks.

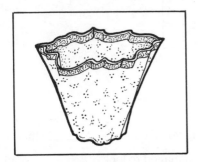

1 This looks ¹___like___ a handkerchief. It is made
²_____ china, and you can use it ³_____ a vase. It
was made ⁴_____ an artist.

2 This was made ⁵_____ a golf ball and some pieces of
paper. You can use it ⁶_____ a paperweight, and it looks
⁷_____ a duck.

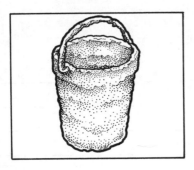

3 This was made ⁸_____ a child, ⁹_____ a plastic
carton, some wire and moss. You can use it ¹⁰_____ a
plant pot.

2 Bus? Car? Train? Boat? Air? Or...?
Say how one can travel from your capital or your home to three
other places.

1 You can travel from _____ to _____ by _____ , or by
_____ or by _____ .

2 _____
_____

3 _____
_____

3 Someone broke the window of a house and stole some silver.
Three people say they saw the robbery, but they have told very
different stories to the police. Complete each description with
prepositions.

WITNESS A: 'He was a man ¹___of___ about 20, ²_____
long dark hair, ³_____ jeans. He was wearing a
mask made ⁴_____ a stocking, and he looked
⁵_____ a gangster. He broke the window
⁶_____ a brick, and escaped ⁷_____ a
bicycle. It looked ⁸_____ a racing bike.'

WITNESS B: 'She was a woman ⁹_____ about 30, ¹⁰_____
short, dark hair, ¹¹_____ a tracksuit. She was
wearing a sort of mask made ¹²_____
cardboard. She broke the window ¹³_____ a
bottle, and escaped ¹⁴_____ a motorcycle. She
drove that motorbike ¹⁵_____ a mad woman!'

WITNESS C: 'He was a man ¹⁶_____ about 40, ¹⁷_____
very little hair, ¹⁸_____ a dark suit. He looked
¹⁹_____ a businessman, and he used his
newspaper ²⁰_____ a sort of mask. He escaped
²¹_____ a large, black car.'

4 Say how you and three other people (family, friends or other
students) travelled to work today.

1 I came to college/school today _____

2 _____

3 _____

4 _____

15 Adjectives + prepositions 1

1

	He was good/kind, etc. *to* my brother (= A PERSON)
	He was good/kind, etc. *about* my brother/ his hat/what my brother did (= AN EVENT OR A SITUATION)
	It was good/kind, etc. *of him to* excuse my brother.

A TV commercial. A cowgirl is speaking to a cowboy.
Write *to, about* or *of* in each blank.

'Ed, darling, what's happened to you? You used to be rude [1]___to___ my parents, but now you're so polite [2]_____ them. You used to be nasty [3]_____ my cooking, but now you're nice [4]_____ it. You used to be unkind [5]_____ my small brother, but now you're very kind [6]_____ him. You were very kind [7]_____ your hat; it really was nice [8]_____ you to keep calm [9]_____ that! You used to be mean [10]_____ the farm workers, but now you're generous [11]_____ them. In fact, you used to be unpleasant [12]_____ everybody and [13]_____ everything, but now you're pleasant [14]_____ everybody and [15]_____ everything. Tell me, Ed, what's happened?'

'What's happened, honey? I've discovered Shavex Shaving Cream! It sure was good [16]_____ you to give me that superb cream for my birthday!'

2

pleased impatient careless patient careful[1] angry	*with* her daughter/the present (= PEOPLE OR THINGS) *about* the match/the heavy traffic (= EVENTS OR SITUATIONS)
right sorry[2] wrong worried	*about* him/the present/the match/the traffic (= PEOPLE, THINGS, EVENTS OR SITUATIONS)

Notes
[1]You can also say *careful of*: Be careful *of* the traffic (= BE CAREFUL THAT IT DOES NOT HARM YOU)
[2]I'm sorry *about* your father (= I AM SORRY THAT HE HAS DIED)
  I'm sorry *for* your father (= I PITY HIM (BECAUSE YOU HAVE TREATED HIM BADLY, ETC.))

Paul and Tina are at a tennis school in Yorkshire.
Paul is writing to his cousin. Fill each blank with *one* word.

1 My tennis racquet's really good. I'm very pleased __with__ __it__ .

2 But I've lost three tennis balls. I'm rather angry _____ __that__ .

3 Now I've only got three. I'll be careful _____ _____ .

4 Our first coach used to shout at us. He was very impatient _____ _____

5 Then he left. We weren't sorry _____ that.

6 The new coach is excellent. He's very patient _____ _____ .

7 At first I thought he was no good, but I was wrong _____ _____ .

8 I won a match today. I'm rather pleased _____ _____ .

9 My big match is tomorrow. I'm not worried _____ _____ .

10 You said that Yorkshire's nice. You were right _____ _____ .

3	to be pleased/worried, etc. *about*	*doing* something *not doing* something

Example
I'm pleased *about being* here, but I'm sorry *about not seeing* you.

Paul is writing to his parents now.
Write *one* word in each blank. Use the verbs in italics.

I *lost* three tennis balls yesterday. I was sorry [1] __about__
__losing__ __them__ . I didn't *find* any of them; I was angry
[2] __about__ __not__ __finding__ __them__ . We have to
wait for our classes. We have to be very patient [3]_____
_____ _____ _____ . I *won* a match today. I
was pleased [4]_____ _____ _____ . I'm
playing in a bigger match tomorrow. I'm not worried
[5]_____ _____ _____ _____ . I haven't
written to you very often. I'm sorry [6]_____ _____
_____ _____ _____ more often.

16 Adjectives + prepositions 2

| 1 | bad
good
quick
slow
clever
efficient | *at* | afraid
fond
proud
sure
tired | *of* | interested
qualified | *in* |
| | | | | | keen | *on* |

Examples

She's good *at* arithmetic but slow *at* algebra.

I'm afraid *of* dogs, but I'm fond *of* cats.

He's interested *in* computers and qualified *in* mathematics.

She's keen *on* sport. She really likes it.

Tina's letter from Yorkshire.

Write *at, of, in* or *on*.

Dear Lucy,

Paul and I can canoe now! At last! So we're very proud

[1] **of** ourselves. Canoeing is a great sport, especially in a

river full of rocks! Of course, we're not very good [2]_____ it

yet, and at first we were really bad [3]_____ it. We fell into

the river at least ten times, I'm sure [4]_____ that. I'm not

afraid [5]_____ the river, but I'm not keen [6]_____

very cold water! Getting into the canoe was rather difficult too,

but we're quite quick [7]_____ that now. So we're enjoying

ourselves, but we're rather tired [8]_____ the rain here. It's

been raining for three days.

Please write. I'll be interested [9]_____ your news.

All the best,

Tina.

2   to be bad *at* /afraid *of* /interested *in*, etc. *doing* something

Examples
He's good *at swimming* and *running*.
She's fond *of driving* fast cars.
He's interested *in helping* other people.
She's keen *on working* with computers.

When Sue first met Tina and Paul in London, she asked them
some questions. Look at her notes and complete her questions.

1 Are you fond ___*of getting up early*___ ?
_____

2 Are you good _____
_____

3 Are you afraid _____
_____

4 Are you keen _____
_____

5 Are you interested _____
_____

1. Get up early.
2. Put up a tent.
3 Try dangerous sports.
4. Meet lots of different people.
5. Learn new skills.

3   What about you, your family and friends? Or what about your
partner? Write sentences like this:
(very keen)   I'm *very keen on* guitar music.
            (.........) is *very keen on taking* photographs
            of wild animals.

(very keen) _____

(qualified) _____

(clever) _____

(rather slow) _____

(good) _____

(very interested) _____

(rather afraid) _____

17 Adjectives + prepositions 3

1

bad good	*for* + noun		capable fond proud sure tired	*of*	+ noun + *doing something*
famous responsible grateful sorry	*for*	+ noun + *doing something*	bored	*with*	

Examples

I'm sorry *for* breaking the dish (= I APOLOGISE)
I'm sorry *for* the animals in the cage (= I PITY THEM)
Fruit is good *for* your health.
She's famous *for* her parties/*for giving* good parties.
He's capable *of* good work/*of doing* good work.
I was bored *with* the talk/*with listening* to the talk.

Find the right ending for each sentence.
Write your answers below.

A Children are usually fond   1 for its beautiful buildings.
B Rome is famous   2 of adults' conversations.
C Children usually get bored   3 for the nerves.
D They also usually get tired   4 of their literature.
E Too much coffee is bad   5 for sad people.
F We feel sorry   6 with reading long books.
G English people are proud   7 of eating sweets.

A __7__ , B ____ , C ____ , D ____ , E ____ , F ____ , G ____

2 Paul and Tina are at a music summer school. Paul is talking to
Vicky, one of the teachers.
Complete the changed versions of their sentences. Sometimes
there are two ways of completing the sentence.

1

I organise the guitar classes.

I'm responsible ___*for (organising) the guitar classes.*___

2

Do you ever think it's boring to do that?

Do you ever get bored _____ ?

3

No, I always enjoy listening to the guitar, so you needn't pity me!

No, I never get tired _____ so you

needn't feel sorry _____ .

4

I like singing, but I don't think my voice is very good.

I'm quite fond _____ , but I'm not very proud _____

5

The singing teacher here gives marvellous classes. She's quite famous!

The singing teacher here is quite famous _____ .

6

Yes, I'm very pleased with all these free lessons.

Yes, I'm grateful _____ .

7

You'd better go to bed early. That will help your voice!

If you go to bed early, that will be good _____ .

8

But it wouldn't help my social life!

But it would be bad _____ .

3

good bad famous capable responsible	*as* + ROLE	**Examples** She's *famous as* a singer (= SHE IS A SINGER, AND SHE IS FAMOUS) Swimming is *good as* a form of exercise (= SWIMMING IS A FORM OF EXERCISE, AND IT IS A GOOD ONE)

What did they say?
Write *as*, *of* or *for* in the blanks.

TED: 'I'm best [1] __*at*__ sports photography. Perhaps one day I'll be famous [2]_____ a
sports photographer.'

TINA: 'People say that swimming is very good [3]_____ you. I'm not bad [4]_____ a
swimmer.'

VICKY: 'I'm responsible, [5]_____ your guitar teacher, [6]_____ giving you finger exercises.
Lack of exercise is bad [7]_____ a guitarist's fingers.'

PAUL: 'I don't think I'll ever be famous [8]_____ my singing. I'm just capable [9]_____
singing a tune. But I'm quite good [10]_____ the class comedian!'

18 Mixed practice

1 Here are some facts about Phil Billy, a singer.
Write *about, as, at, for* or *to* in column 2.

1 He's very good	_at_	singing.
2 But he's also good	_____	an actor.
3 He's very good	_____	his family.
4 He says coffee is bad	_____	his voice.
5 He's always good	_____	any problems during recording.
6 He's just rather bad	_____	arriving on time.

2 A hotel receptionist is talking about her work.
In the blanks, write adjectives from the list on the right.
Use each adjective *once*.

You have to be quite ¹____ *good* ____ at speaking English,
French, Spanish and German. You are ²_____ for the
keys to the rooms, and you have to be ³_____ about
writing down telephone messages exactly. Also, you must be
really ⁴_____ at keeping the list of guests up to date.
Some guests are not very easy or pleasant, but you have to be
⁵_____ with the difficult ones, you must at least seem
to be ⁶_____ in their problems, and of course you
must be ⁷_____ to all of them! Naturally, there are
times when I get ⁸_____ of answering all their
questions, and at the end of a difficult day I sometimes feel
quite ⁹_____ of screaming, but I never really get
¹⁰_____ with the work.

bored
capable
careful
efficient
good
interested
patient
polite
responsible
tired

3 Apologies. Two friends are talking.
Choose the right endings from the list below the dialogue.

Hullo! I'm so sorry [1] _d_ . It's been good [2] _____ .

I was quite worried [3] _____ . I'll be interested [4] _____ .

I crashed my bike into a pedestrian. At first, I thought he was hurt, but I was wrong [5] _____ .

So? What happened? Tell me!

Just be patient [6] _____ . A policeman came along and he said I was responsible [7] _____ , because I'd been careless [8] _____ .

Poor you! I'm beginning to feel sorry [9] _____ .

Well, I told the policeman that I was very sorry [10] _____ .

And you really were sorry, I'm sure [11] _____ .

Yes, so for the next half hour, please be nice [12] _____ .

a about the accident	d about being late	g for the accident	j with me
b about that	e about signalling	h of that	k in your explanation
c about you	f for you	i to me	l of you to wait

19 Verbs + prepositions 1

1

listen speak/talk write belong happen	to	
ask wait pay look	for	(= TRY TO FIND)

look	at	
look	after	(= TAKE CARE OF)

Examples
Something nice happened *to* me today.
I'm looking *for* my hat.
I'm looking *at* some interesting photographs.
I'm looking *after* their baby today.

Ted is telling Sue about a terrible restaurant he went to.
Write a preposition in each blank.

Just listen ^{1}__**to**__ this. To begin with, I had to wait twenty

minutes ^{2}_____ the waitress. When I asked her

^{3}_____ the menu, she had to go and look ^{4}_____ it;

there was only one, and something had happened ^{5}_____

it. Then, when I spoke ^{6}_____ her she didn't listen

^{7}_____ me, so she brought some cheese which I didn't want.

I hadn't asked ^{8}_____ it, but she wanted me to pay

^{9}_____ it! The restaurant belongs ^{10}_____ Tamara

Lane, the TV cookery expert. I shall write ^{11}_____ her. The

waitresses really should look ^{12}_____ the customers

better.

2

speak/talk write complain	(to someone)	about	+ noun + *doing something*
tell	someone		
think/dream			

Examples
She talked *about* Spain/*about travelling* in Spain.
He's thinking *about* a holiday abroad/*about going* abroad.

Note
Tell must take an indirect object:
Tell *us* about your holiday.
(NOT: Tell about your holiday.)

In the terrible restaurant.
Complete the descriptions. Use the verbs in italics.

1 Where's the waitress? I've no bread.

   A is going to complain   _to the waitress about having no bread._

2 One day I'll *have* my own restaurant.

   B is dreaming _____

3 I've *found* a piece of string in my soup! The waitress should know about this!

   C is going to tell _____

4 The chef here doesn't know how to *cook* vegetables. I want to tell him ...

   D wants to talk _____

5 I think the Health Inspector should *close* this restaurant.

   I must send him a letter.

   E is going to write _____

6 Perhaps I should *look* for another job.

   The waitress is thinking _____

3 Write some sentences about your last summer holiday, or ask the
questions and write about your partner's holiday.

1 Did you speak to anyone interesting? About what?

   _____

2 Did you buy anything special? How much did you pay for it?

   I paid _____

3 Did you or anyone else complain about anything? To whom?

   _____

4 Did you write to anyone? About what?

   _____

5 What might you do during your next summer holiday?

   I'm thinking _____

43

20 Verbs + prepositions 2

1

run/bump	*into*	I *ran into* a friend yesterday (= WE MET BY CHANCE)
run/bump/crash	*into*	The car *ran into* the wall (= IT HAD AN ACCIDENT)
run	*over*	The car *ran over* a cat (= IT KNOCKED THE CAT DOWN AND DROVE OVER IT)
run/drive, etc.	*after*	The policeman *ran after* the thief (= HE FOLLOWED THE THIEF WHILE RUNNING)
catch up	*with*	The policeman ran fast and *caught up with* the thief (= THE POLICEMAN WAS BEHIND AT FIRST, BUT THEN HE REACHED THE SAME PLACE AS THE THIEF)

Tina and Paul took part in a cross-country bicycle race.
Complete the description of what happened.

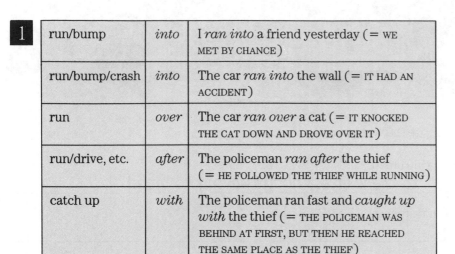

1 Another cyclist _____ran into_____ Tina.

2 So Tina nearly _____ a small boy.

3 The father _____ her.

4 But he couldn't _____ her.

5 Paul nearly _____ a tree.

6 After the race, Tina _____ a friend from her college.

2

shout throw	*at*	(= ANGRILY) (= WANTING TO HIT SOMEONE OR SOMETHING) They shouted *at* the thief and threw stones *at* him.
shout throw	*to*	(= WANTING THE OTHER PERSON TO HEAR) (= SO THAT THE OTHER PERSON CAN CATCH) She shouted *to* me that I should come upstairs, and threw the key down *to* me.
laugh smile stare point	*at*	First the children stared and pointed *at* the comedian; then they laughed *at* his jokes.
wave	*at/to*	The film star waved *at/to* the crowd.

Find a suitable ending in column 3 for each sentence.

1 I might	stare	a to a small child.
2	wave	b at a strange person.
3	throw a ball	c at a good joke.
4	shout	d at a friend in another car.
5	laugh	e at something I wanted to buy.
6	point	f to a friend in another room.

Answers: 1 __b__ , 2 _____ , 3 _____ , 4 _____ , 5 _____ , 6 _____

3 Things that happened at the bicycle race.
Write prepositions from Exercises 1 and 2 in the spaces.

1 Tina shouted ¹__to__ the small boy that he should stay

off the road.

2 The boy's father was very angry, so he shouted ²_____

Tina and threw a stone ³_____ her.

3 The other people stared ⁴_____ him and pointed

⁵_____ Tina.

4 The father wanted a police car to drive ⁶_____ Tina, but

the policemen only smiled ⁷_____ him.

5 When Tina saw her friend, she waved ⁸_____ her and

shouted 'Hullo!' ⁹_____ her.

21 Verbs + prepositions 3

1

		+ noun	+ *doing*	
apply	*for*	✓	–	
apologise		✓	✓	
reply	*to*	✓	–	
look forward		✓	✓	
hear	*from*	✓	–	(= RECEIVE NEWS FROM SOMEONE IN A LETTER, BY TELEPHONE, ETC.)
consist	*of*	✓	✓	
call	*on*	✓	–	(= VISIT SOMEONE FORMALLY)
drop in		✓	–	(= VISIT SOMEONE INFORMALLY OR UNEXPECTEDLY)

Examples
He apologised *for* his mistake/*for making* that mistake.
I'm looking forward *to* my new job/*to starting* my new job.
A knife consists *of* a handle and a blade.
His job as a tourist guide consists *of taking* tourists round the town and *answering* their questions.

Note
Ask, answer, ring and *telephone* take no preposition:
    They couldn't *answer the teacher.*
    I'll *ring/telephone your secretary.*

■ Find a suitable ending in column 2 for each sentence.

Usually:
1 We reply
2 We look forward
3 We are pleased when we hear
4 We also enjoy telephoning
5 We drop in
6 We apologise
7 We apply
8 Our lives consist

a from our friends.
b for being late.
c on old friends and relatives.
d to people's letters.
e of work, home life, and leisure.
f to going on holiday.
g our friends.
h for jobs, or places on courses, etc.

1 __d__ , 2 ____ , 3 ____ , 4 ____ , 5 ____ , 6 ____ , 7 ____ , 8 ____

2

to be	employed qualified involved	*in*	+ noun (e.g. medicine)	*as*	(ROLE OR POSITION) *(e.g. a doctor)*
			+ *doing* (e.g. teaching)		

Examples
He's employed *in* the oil industry *as* an engineer.
She's involved *in* travelling to many countries *as* a business executive.

Tina decided to apply for a spring holiday job at the music school. In each blank, write a preposition from Exercise 1 or 2, or write a dash (−).

Dear Sirs,

I would like to apply ¹ ___for___ the job of spring holiday

helper, which you advertised recently. I apologise ² _____

applying rather late. When I telephoned ³ _____ your

secretary, she said I could still apply.

I am not employed ⁴ _____ teaching, but I am qualified

⁵ _____ an advanced guitar player (Grade 8) and I am

involved ⁶ _____ teaching the guitar ⁷ _____ a helper

in a youth club. My work in the youth club consists ⁸ _____

helping the staff generally and some teaching.

I hope you will be interested in my application, and am looking

forward ⁹ _____ hearing ¹⁰ _____ you.

Yours faithfully,

Tina Brown

3 Write your own application for a job you would like.

_____
_____
_____
_____
_____
_____
_____

22 Verbs + prepositions 4

1

| concentrate
decide
depend
rely
insist
work | *on* | + noun
+ *doing* | **Examples**
She was concentrating *on* her book/*on reading* her book.
They were working *on* the car. (e.g. making or repairing it)
They were working *on getting* the car ready by 5.00. (= WERE MAKING AN EFFORT TO ACHIEVE THIS) |

Paul has made this list of things that he will do and will not do when he returns home.
Write what he is thinking.

1 I'll insist __on getting my dictionary back from Bill.__

2 I'll decide _____

3 I'll work _____

4 I'll concentrate _____

5 I won't rely _____

1 Dictionary. Get back from Bill.
2 Possible career. Decide.
3 must improve my essay techniques.
4 Must pass exams.
5 Not revise at the last minute!

2 All these verbs need a direct object before the preposition.

	Direct object			**Examples**
invite	someone	*to*	+ noun	They invited *me to* their party. She borrowed *a book from* a friend. They accused *him of* the crime/*of stealing* the money. I congratulate *you on* your success/*on winning* the race. This house reminds *me of* my home. They reminded *her about not leaving* her bag in the car. They warned *us about* the danger/*about* swimming near the rocks.
provide	someone	*with*	
borrow	something	*from*	
accuse	someone	*of*	+ noun + *(not) doing*
blame	someone/something	*for*	
congratulate	someone	*on*	
protect	someone	*from*	
spend	something	*on*	
remind	someone	*about*	
warn	someone	*about*	

Tina is writing to her cousin about a lesson in windsurfing.
Write a preposition in each blank.

You certainly can't accuse me ^{1}___of___ being lazy! One of
the instructors here invited me ^{2}_____ a windsurfing
lesson, after a whole day's tennis, and I said 'Yes!' Of course, at
home I would have to spend a lot of money ^{3}_____ buying
equipment, but I borrowed a wet suit ^{4}_____ the Centre.
Naturally, they provide learners ^{5}_____ the sailboard. I
didn't need a crash helmet to protect me ^{6}_____ the
sailboard. Really, the sailboard needed to be protected
^{7}_____ me! The instructor reminded me ^{8}_____ the
correct position of my feet, and warned me ^{9}_____ not
letting go of the boom, but ...! Anyway, he didn't blame me
^{10}_____ falling in, and he even congratulated me
^{11}_____ not falling through the sail!

boom

wet
suit

sai

3 Finish these sentences. Write a direct object if necessary, the
preposition, and the verb in brackets in its correct form.

1 When Tina fell in, the instructor didn't blame __her for__
__falling_____ in. (fall)

2 Tina insisted _____

again. (try)

3 The instructor reminded _____

_____ on the middle of the board. (get)

4 He also warned _____ on to

it. (not jump)

5 This time she concentrated _____

_____ the boom firmly. (hold)

6 He congratulated _____

so quickly. (learn)

23 Mixed practice

Charles works in the personnel department of a large company. How does he spend the day? In each blank, write a preposition, or a dash (–) if there should be no preposition.

For much of the day, Charles listens ¹ __to__ people. They tell ² _____ him ³ _____ their problems or their ambitions. He answers ⁴ _____ their questions. Sometimes they complain ⁵ _____ him ⁶ _____ their bosses. That's difficult for Charles. He can't reply easily ⁷ _____ a person who asks ⁸ _____ him ⁹ _____ help about a bad boss. Charles says: 'My work consists ¹⁰ _____ listening a lot, saying a little, and smiling ¹¹ _____ nearly everyone who comes in!'

Charles is on the telephone.
Find the right ending for each sentence. Write your answers below.

1 So two weeks ago you applied	a to your letter.
2 But you still haven't heard	b for that.
3 It seems that we didn't reply	c for a job with us.
4 Well, I do apologise	d from us.
5 Actually, I'm sure that we answered	e of lying!
6 I remember, we wrote	f your letter.
7 No! I'm not accusing you	g to you three days ago.

1 _C_ , 2 ___ , 3 ___ , 4 ___ , 5 ___ , 6 ___ , 7 ___

3 Charles is still on the telephone.
Find the right ending for each sentence. Write your answers below.

1 Yes! I'm listening	a in starting our new computer.
2 You see, we've been very involved	b to seeing you.
3 We've been concentrating	c with a new application form.
4 Oh, you're qualified	d on us tomorrow to collect it?
5 Anyway, we must provide you	e as a computer programmer.
6 Could you drop in	f on learning to use it.
7 And this time you can depend	g us.
8 So I look forward	h to you.
9 And thank you for telephoning	i on us to reply.

1 _h_ , 2 ___ , 3 ___ , 4 ___ , 5 ___ , 6 ___ , 7 ___ , 8 ___ ,

9 ___

4 After a concert. People are waiting to see the singer Contessa when she comes out of the theatre.
Write a preposition or a dash (−) in each space.

1 I just want to look __*at*__ her. I've been waiting _____ her since 6.00.

6 Why isn't she here? What's happened _____ her?

7 I'm going to ask _____ her _____ a photograph. Anyway, I'll try to speak _____ her.

2 A lot of rude people will stare _____ her and shout _____ her. But *I'm* just going to smile _____ her and wave _____ her.

8 Those two enormous men protect her _____ the crowds; they look _____ her.

3 I spent a lot of money _____ my ticket, and I'm going to insist _____ seeing her.

9 What? She's gone! She left by another door! I'm going to complain _____ the theatre _____ that!

4 I want to congratulate her _____ a marvellous show. But will she listen _____ me?

10 Ah, well. She was probably tired. You can't blame her _____ being tired.

5 That enormous car belongs _____ her. How much did she pay _____ it, I wonder?

24 Usual phrases 1

1

			Examples
a	visit	*to*	his visit *to* Africa/*to* the doctor.
	plan	*for*	our plans *for* our holiday/*for* you.
	meeting	*with*	The students had a meeting *with* the professor.
		between	There was a meeting *between* the students and the professor.
		of	There was a meeting *of* the new students.
a	book letter talk/lecture programme (on TV or radio)	*on*[1] *about*[2]	a book *on/about* Brazil; *on/about travelling* in Brazil some advice *on/about* the problem; *on/about solving* the problem
some	advice ideas		

Notes

[1]We usually use *on* for rather formal or specialised books, or when we are using a rather formal style of English:

The professor wrote a letter to the newspaper *on* the country's economic situation.

[2]We usually use *about* for more informal or general books, or when we are using a more informal style of English:

My cousin wrote me a letter *about* his holiday.

Ted has made a list of things he must do when he returns to London. He's telling Sue about them.
Fill in the blanks.

'When I get back, I've got to attend a meeting [1]__of__ the Photographic Society; prepare plans [2]_____ the Society's visit [3]_____ Cambridge; send the Tourist Board a letter [4]_____ our visit; get some advice [5]_____ transport; and find a good book [6]_____ architectural photography. Do you have any ideas [7]_____ unusual buildings we can photograph? No? Oh well, there's a TV programme [8]_____ Cambridge the night before we go. Oh, and I want to arrange a meeting [9]_____ the University's Camera Club. Well, all that will keep me busy!'

> Photographic Society meeting
>
> N.B. Society visit Cambridge. must:
> 1 Prepare plans
> 2 Write Cambridge Tourist Board
> 3 Trains, etc. - get advice
> 4 Architectural photography - find good book
> 5 Unusual buildings in Cambridge. Sue: any ideas?
> 6 30 July: Watch TV - "Cambridge Architecture."
> 7 University Camera Club: try to meet members?

2

a	question reply/answer	to about	**Examples** That was his question *to* her *about* the journey/*about planning* the journey.
	reason need	*for*	Is there any need *for* silence/*for being* silent?
	cause result cost/price way	*of*	His success was the result *of* hard work/*of working* hard. This is my way *of* frying eggs.
	rise/increase fall/decrease	*in*	Last year there was an increase *in* the number of tourists here.

Some time later, Ted received this letter from a coach company. Fill in the blanks.

Dear Sir,

This letter is in reply [1] **to** your letter of 15 August. The reason [2] _____ the rise [3] _____ the cost [4] _____ hiring a coach is the recent increase [5] _____ the price [6] _____ petrol. This increase, as you know, has been the result [7] _____ problems in the oil industry. We do understand the need [8] _____ inexpensive transport for your society, and we feel sure that you will not find a cheaper way [9] _____ taking your members to Cambridge. Of course, if there is a fall [10] _____ the price of petrol, there will be a decrease [11] _____ our charge to you.

Yours faithfully,

D A Cotten

Comfort Coaches Ltd.

3 Complete this list about yourself, or a partner. Use prepositions from the tables. For example:
I would be interested in a meeting *with* the President.

I would be interested in these things:

a meeting _____ ;   a TV programme _____ ;

a visit _____ ;   a talk _____ .

a book _____ .

25 Usual phrases 2

to be	*at*	work school college university		to	go come	*to*	work school college university church bed
		in/at church *in* hospital *in* bed *at* home				*to/into* hospital	
						home	

Examples
He's *at* work today, although it's a holiday.
My sister is going *to* college next year.
The children are *in* bed. They went *to* bed early.
Father's *at* home. He *came home* a few minutes ago.

Note
With all the words above (except *work*) we use *the* or *a* if
we are referring to a particular school, church, bed, etc.
     He was *in the bed* by the window.
     A doctor *in the hospital* spoke to us.
     Father went *to the home* of some friends this evening.

What they said at a party.
Put one or two words, or a dash (–) in each blank.

TINA: 'Yes, my brother's still ¹___*at*___ school, but he wants to go ²_____ college when

he's eighteen. I'm ³_____ university myself. I'm ⁴_____ university in the west of

England. Guess which!'

TED: 'After my football accident I had to go ⁵_____ hospital for a while. I was ⁶_____

hospital for three days, and then I spent another week ⁷_____ bed ⁸_____ home.'

PAUL: 'I'm hoping to have a job next summer. There are jobs ⁹_____ hospital near my home. I

go ¹⁰_____ school which helps you to find summer jobs.'

SUE: 'In thirty-six hours' time I'll be back ¹¹_____ work in London. I'm rather looking forward

to going ¹²_____ home. I'm going ¹³_____ church tomorrow. I'd like to go

¹⁴_____ church where the singing is really good.'

2

to have (something)	*for*	breakfast lunch, etc.
to be/go, etc.	*on*	holiday business
to be/speak, etc.	*on*	the telephone/phone the radio TV
to go/come	*for*	a run a swim, etc.

The manager of a young tennis star is having a telephone
conversation with a reporter.
Write a preposition in each blank.

1 Yes, Rob is here ___*on*___ holiday, not _____

   business.

2 No, he can't speak to you _____ the phone.

3 Yes, he did go _____ a run this morning.

4 He had two oranges and a boiled egg _____ breakfast.

5 No, I don't know what he had _____ dinner yesterday.

6 Yes, he might go _____ a swim later today.

7 You'll see him _____ TV tomorrow, and he'll have an

   interview _____ the radio on Monday.

3

Complete each of these questions with one or two words.
Then answer them yourself, or ask a partner to answer them.

1 Where would you most like to go _____ holiday?

2 What do you most enjoy doing _____ home?

3 What do/did you most enjoy _____ school?

4 What would you most like to have _____ lunch or dinner

   on your birthday?

5 How much time do you usually spend _____ telephone

   in a week?

6 Have you ever been _____ a swim in the moonlight?

26 Usual phrases 3

1

a	book, play, etc. painting, drawing, etc. song, symphony, etc.	*by*	Shakespeare Picasso Mozart

These sentences are nonsense! Rearrange the words in columns
3 and 5, and write down true sentences.

1 Hamlet	is a(n)	painting	by	Lennon and McCartney.
2 Yesterday		novel		Mozart.
3 War and Peace		play		Leonardo da Vinci.
4 The Mona Lisa		opera		Michelangelo.
5 David		statue		Tolstoy.
6 Don Giovanni		song		Shakespeare.

1 *Hamlet is a play by Shakespeare.* _____

2 _____

3 _____

4 _____

5 _____

6 _____

2

in	danger love (with)
indoors	

out of	danger work order	(= WITHOUT A JOB) He lost his job, and is now *out of work*. (= NOT FUNCTIONING) I dropped the telephone and now it's *out of order*.
out of doors		

Complete the sentences below to fill in the words in this puzzle.

1 Office workers spend most of their time ___ . (one word)

2 An unemployed person is ___ . (three words)

3 If a person has a temperature of 42°, his/her life is ___ . (two words)

4 Most people are ___ when they marry. (two words)

5 A farmer spends a lot of his time ___ . (three words)

6 If your telephone is broken, it is out of ___ . (one word)

3	*on*	purpose
		my/your, etc. own

by	mistake
	myself/yourself, etc.

in	charge
	a hurry

up to	date	(= MODERN)
		an up to date dictionary
out of		(= NOT MODERN, NO LONGER SUITABLE OR CORRECT)

Fill in the blanks to complete this information.

Paul wants to move to a college with a modern computing department, where there is [1] **up to** date equipment. He says: 'I tried to ring the college for information, but I got the wrong number, because the telephone directory was [2]_____ date. The person who answered was rather angry, so I said, "Look, I got your number [3]_____ mistake. I certainly haven't bothered you [4]_____ purpose."'

Tina is [5]_____ a hurry to leave university. She would like a job where she is [6]_____ charge of the arrangements for musicians from abroad. She would like to live [7]_____ her own for some time, but she says, 'I probably couldn't pay the rent [8]_____ myself.'

4 Answer these questions about yourself, or ask a partner to answer them.
Five years from now, what do you think?
1 Will you spend most of your time indoors or out of doors?
2 Will you be in charge of any other people?
3 Will you be in love?
4 Will you be living on your own?
Begin your sentences like this:
I think I will...
   ... thinks he/she will...

1 _____

2 _____

3 _____

4 _____

27 Mixed practice

1 Lee is in her first job. She is in the office, writing a letter to a friend. Complete the sentences from her letter, using each item below *once* only. Use – if there should be no word.

(–) at for for in in into on out of

1 Three of the people here were ____*at*____ college or university just before they joined the company.

2 Two of the people here go _____ a swim before work every day.

3 I always stay _____ bed until the last minute, so I only have a cup of tea _____ breakfast.

4 At the end of the day, most of the staff go straight _____ home, but I'd like to do something more exciting!

5 We can't use the computer today because it's _____ order.

6 My neighbour's having a long conversation _____ the phone.

7 One of the men has had to go _____ hospital for an operation.

8 Some of the staff are going to visit him while he's _____ hospital.

2 Write the opposite of the expressions in italics. Fill in each blank with *one* word.

1 Lee isn't *at home* today. She's ____*at*____ ____*work*____ .

2 There hasn't been a *rise in* the number of unemployed people. There has been a _____ _____ the number.

3 You didn't do that *by mistake!* You did it _____ _____ .

4 He didn't want to be *indoors* on that lovely day. He wanted to be _____ _____ _____ .

5 She didn't go to Hawaii *on holiday*. She went _____ _____ .

6 Last month there was an *increase in* the price of fruit, but this month there has been a _____ _____ the price.

7 This list of prices is *out of date*. I need a list that is _____ _____ _____ .

3 These are three sets of headings from a magazine. Complete the explanations. Write a preposition in each blank.

1 The Minister in charge ___of___ medical research, in a reply _____ questions, said: 'We do not know the cause _____ this new illness. We must find a way _____ curing it, and there is a need _____ research. But we must not act _____ a hurry. This is an international problem, and we cannot act _____ ourselves.'

2 This article _____ Helen Venables is _____ her voyage round the world _____ her own. The low cost _____ the voyage was the result _____ gifts from several large organisations.

3 A reporter has had a meeting _____ 'Rocket' Ronson, who is on a visit _____ England. Ronson talked about his plans _____ a new tournament, and explained his reasons _____ wanting a new tournament.

> (1) Mysterious new illness.
> Minister responsible for medical research answers questions. 'We do not know causes. Research is needed. Cannot act quickly. Must act with other nations.'

> (2) Helen Venables writes.
> 'How I sailed round the world alone, for £1,000.' Big organisations were generous.

> (3) 'Rocket' Ronson, world's No.1 tennis champion, in England.
> Planning a new international tournament. Why?

4 How would you feel about doing these things? Complete each question with a preposition. Then answer the questions yourself, or ask another student to answer them. For example: How would you feel about staying at home for three days without going out?
Tick (✓) one box in reply to each question.

	O.K.	Not O.K.	It depends
1 Spend three days __at__ home without going out.			
2 Spend three nights _____ _____ doors, in a tent.			
3 Cook a dinner for four people _____ yourself.			
4 Get dressed for an important party _____ a hurry.			
5 Pay a visit _____ a house full of people whom you don't know.			
6 Write a magazine article _____ someone you know.			

Answer key

1 Where? 1 (pages 6 and 7)

1
2 in 3 at 4 on the corner of
5 next to 6 opposite 7 far from
8 far from 9 at 10 opposite
11 next to

2
1 on top of 3 on 4 at the top of
5 above 6 below

2 Where? 2 (pages 8 and 9)

1
2 at the back of 3 on the left
4 on the right of 5 at the front

2
2 outside 3 round 4 in front of
5 beside 6 behind

3
2 on 3 above 4 Through 5 on
6 on 7 in a corner of 8 in

3 Where? 3 (pages 10 and 11)

1
1 False. Portsmouth is north of St
Helen's. 2 True 3 True 4 False.
Portsmouth is on the coast of England.
5 False. Cowes is north of Newport.

2
2 east 3 in 4 on 5 in 6 north
7 from 8 in the north/in the north-
west

3
2 in 3 in 4 on 5 on 6 in
7 on

4
2 by 3 on 4 on top of 5 off
6 in 7 off

4 Mixed practice (pages 12 and 13)

1

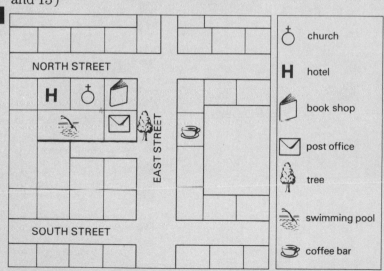

2

1
1 at the top of 2 at the bottom
3 on the left 4 on the right
5 on/on top of 6 beside/next to
7 above 8 below 9 in/inside
10 outside

3
2 above/over 3 on 4 behind
5 on 6 in 7 at 8 on
9 off/near 10 from 11 near
12 from 13 far from 14 on
15 north/north-west 16 in the
north of

5 Direction 1 (pages 14 and 15)

1
2 from 3 along 4 towards
5 past 6 as far as 7 left 8 into

2
2 lift 3 stairs 4 stairs
5 passage/corridor 6 door
7 cupboard

3
2 up 3 along 4 into 5 out of
6 down 7 through 8 into

6 Direction 2 (pages 16 and 17)

1
2 through 3 along 4 over
5 round 6 across 7 under

2
2 round 3 over 4 along
5 through 6 across 7 under

3
2 into 3 across 4 out of 5 over
6 across 7 over 8 on to 9 off
10 on to

7 Direction 3 (pages 18 and 19)

1
2 in 3 to 4 to 5 to 6 at/in
7 to

2

1
2 to 3 to 4 at 5 to 6 in
7 for 8 at

2
2 as far as 3 through/into 4 into
5 out of 6 towards 7 to 8 from

8 Mixed practice (pages 20 and 21)

1
2 through 3 past 4 round
5 over/across 6 across/over
7 round 8 along 9 through
10 into 11 through 12 along
13 towards/as far as 14 into
15 towards 16 past 17 over/
across 18 as far as

2
2 over 3 on to 4 into
5 through 6 in 7 out of 8 off
9 on 10 down 11 from
12 across 13 up 14 into

3
2 in 3 to 4 for 5 to
6 in/at 7 to

9 When? 1 (pages 22 and 23)

1
2 in 3 at 4 on 5 in 6 in
7 on 8 in 9 in 10 on 11 on
12 on 13 in

2
3 – 4 On 5 – 6 in 7 –

3
2 at 3 at 4 in 5 In 6 at 7 –
8 – 9 at

10 When? 2 (pages 24 and 25)

1
2 for 3 since 4 after 5 from,
to/until/till 6 during 7 for 8 for
9 for 10 since

2
2 by 3 to 4 until 5 by 6 until
7 by 8 to

11 Mixed practice (pages 26 and 27)

1
2 before 3 by 4 from
5 to/until/till 6 until/till 7 at
8 in 9 from 10 to/until/till
11 after

2
2 since 3 from 4 to/until/till
5 during 6 for 7 for 8 – 9 on
10 – 11 for/– 12 – 13 until/till

A suggested text: Contessa was born in Leeds on 10 May 1963. She went to school in 1968 and stayed there until 1979, and hated it. In 1973 she began singing in a church choir, and stayed in the choir for five years. By 1978 she had already made three records – for the church! In 1980 she began singing with a local group called The Pebbles, and stayed with them until 1982. On 4 August 1981 she sang in a show in Brighton. A Mammoth Records producer was in the audience. Two weeks later, she signed a contract with Mammoth Records. She has been under contract with Mammoth since then. In 1986 and 1987 she had two golden discs. Contessa says, 'I have been singing for other people for 15 years, but I really sing for myself.' She plans to make a third gold disc (by her 25th birthday!) I checked the charts last Saturday, and it seems possible.

12 How? (pages 28 and 29)

1 2 by   3 on the   4 by   5 by   6 by   7 on the   8 by   9 in the   10 on   11 in his   12 by   13 on the/that   14 by/on a   15 on an/his

2 1 out of   2 of   3 by   4 with   5 by   6 out of   7 of   8 with   9 out of   10 of   11 by   12 with

13 What are they like? (pages 30 and 31)

1 2 curly hair   3 a white blouse   4 a guitar   5 at least 25   6 a small moustache   7 a small black hat   8 a walking stick   9 about 16   10 dark glasses   11 an amazing hairstyle   12 a strange bag

2 2 like   3 as   4 like   5 like   6 like   7 as   8 like   9 as   10 like   11 like

14 Mixed practice (pages 32 and 33)

1 2 of   3 as   4 by   5 out of   6 as   7 like   8 by   9 out of   10 as

2 2 with   3 in   4 out of   5 like   6 with   7 on   8 like   9 of   10 with   11 in   12 of   13 with   14 on   15 like   16 of   17 with   18 in   19 like   20 as   21 in

15 Adjectives + prepositions 1 (pages 34 and 35)

1 2 to   3 about   4 about   5 to   6 to   7 about   8 of   9 about   10 to   11 to   12 to   13 about   14 to   15 about   16 of

2 2 about them/that   3 with them   4 with us   5 about   6 with us   7 about him/that   8 about it/that   9 about it/that   10 about it/that

3 3 about waiting for them   4 about winning it   5 about playing in it   6 about not writing to you

16 Adjectives + prepositions 2 (pages 36 and 37)

1 2 at   3 at   4 of   5 of   6 on   7 at   8 of   9 in

2 2 at putting up a tent?   3 of trying dangerous sports?   4 on meeting lots of different people?   5 in learning new skills?

17 Adjectives + prepositions 3 (pages 38 and 39)

1 A 7   B 1   C 6   D 2   E 3   F 5   G 4

2 2 with (doing) that?   3 of (listening to) the guitar; for me!   4 of singing; of my voice   5 for her marvellous singing lessons/for giving marvellous singing lessons   6 for all these free lessons   7 for your voice   8 for my social life!

3 2 as   3 for   4 as   5 as   6 for   7 for   8 for   9 of   10 as

18 Mixed practice (pages 40 and 41)

1 2 as   3 to   4 for   5 about   6 at

2 2 responsible   3 careful   4 efficient   5 patient   6 interested   7 polite   8 tired   9 capable   10 bored

3 2 l   3 c   4 k   5 b   6 j   7 g   8 e   9 f   10 a   11 b/h   12 i

19 Verbs + prepositions 1 (pages 42 and 43)

1 2 for   3 for   4 for   5 to   6 to   7 to   8 for   9 for   10 to   11 to   12 after

2 2 about having her own restaurant   3 the waitress about finding a piece of string in his soup   4 to the chef about cooking vegetables   5 to the Health Inspector about closing this/the restaurant   6 about looking for another job

20 Verbs + prepositions 2 (pages 44 and 45)

1 2 ran over   3 ran after   4 catch up with   5 ran/crashed/bumped into   6 ran/bumped into

2 2 d   3 a   4 f   5 c   6 e

3 2 at   3 at   4 at   5 at   6 after   7 at   8 at/to   9 to

21 Verbs + prepositions 3 (pages 46 and 47)

1 2 f   3 a   4 g   5 c   6 b   7 h   8 e

2 2 for   3 –   4 in   5 as   6 in   7 as   8 of   9 to   10 from

22 Verbs + prepositions 4 (pages 48 and 49)

1 2 on a possible career   3 on (improving) my essay techniques   4 on (passing) the exams   5 on revising at the last minute

2 2 to/(for)   3 on   4 from   5 with   6 from   7 from   8 about   9 about   10 for   11 on

3 2 on trying   3 her about getting   4 her about not jumping   5 on holding   6 her on learning

23 Mixed practice (pages 50 and 51)

1 2 –   3 about   4 –   5 to   6 about   7 to   8 –   9 for   10 of   11 at

2 2 d   3 a   4 b   5 f   6 g   7 e

3 2 a   3 f   4 e   5 c   6 d   7 i   8 b   9 g

4 1 for   2 at, at, at, at, to   3 on, on   4 on, to   5 to, for   6 to   7 –, for, to   8 from, after   9 to, about   10 for

24 Usual phrases 1 (pages 52 and 53)

■ 2 for 3 to 4 about 5 on/about
6 on/about 7 on/about
8 on/about 9 with

■ 2 for 3 in 4 of 5 in 6 of
7 of 8 for 9 of 10 in 11 in

25 Usual phrases 2 (pages 54 and 55)

■ 2 to 3 at 4 at a 5 to 6 in
7 in 8 at 9 in a 10 to a 11 at
12 – 13 to 14 to a

■ 1 on, on 2 on 3 for 4 for
5 for 6 for 7 on, on

■ 1 on 2 at 3 at 4 for
5 on the 6 for

26 Usual phrases 3 (pages 56 and 57)

■ 1 Hamlet – play – Shakespeare
2 Yesterday – song – the Beatles
3 War and Peace – novel – Tolstoy
4 The Mona Lisa – painting –
Leonardo da Vinci 5 David – statue
– Michelangelo 6 Don Giovanni –
opera – Mozart

■ 1 indoors 2 out of work 3 in
danger 4 in love 5 out of doors
6 order

■ 2 out of 3 by 4 on 5 in 6 in
7 on 8 by

27 Mixed practice (pages 58 and 59)

■ 2 for 3 in, for 4 – 5 out of
6 on 7 to/into 8 in

■ 2 fall in/decrease in 3 on
purpose 4 out of doors 5 on
business 6 decrease in/fall in 7 up
to date

■ 1 to, of, of, for, in, by 2 by, about/on,
on, of, of 3 with, to, for, for

4 2 out of 3 by 4 in 5 to
6 about/on

Pearson Education Limited
Edinburgh Gate, Harlow,
Essex CM20 2JE, England
and Associated Companies throughout the world.

www.longman-elt.com

First published 1990
Twelfth impression 2000

Set in 10/12pt Linotron Century Light

Printed in Malaysia, PP

ISBN 0-582-00994-4

Illustrated by Kathy Baxendale, Ray Burrows, Hardlines
Norah Fitzwater, Dave Parkins, Liz Roberts and Chris Ryley.